Printed By Createspace, An Amazon.com Company

16364154R00072

Printed in Great Britain
by Amazon